Overcoming
Codependency:

How to Have Healthy Relationships and Be Codependent No More

By Frank James

Table of Contents

Introduction

Codependency can be a serious problem which is also, unfortunately, difficult to recognize in one's self. Whether or not you know for sure you are a codependent person, there are likely at least one or two unhealthy habits you have that you would be better off without. If you are experiencing stress or unhappiness in your relationship for any reason, there are things you can do to resolve those problems or create a better life for yourself. This book may help you discover some of the things you can do.

If you have never heard the phrase "codependency" before or if you are still mostly unfamiliar with what exactly it means, read this brief overview of codependency before moving on to the next chapter:

Overview of Codependency

Codependency is a recognized psychological condition that affects a great number of people. However, unlike most other psychological conditions, this one only occurs within the context of a relationship. That is, you cannot be codependent by yourself. Of course, you can have such a personality that easily becomes codependent even while you are not currently in a relationship and this will quickly become expressed as soon as you are involved in any relationship.

Another important thing to note about codependency is that it can occur in any type of relationship, not just romantic. A mother and her daughter or a pair of platonic friends can be stuck in a codependent relationship just as easily as two people who are romantically involved.

This means that when you are reading through the next chapters, you should not only be considering your romantic relationship but your relationships with family members, coworkers, friends, and anyone else you deal with on a regular basis. Doing so will help you to better identify any codependent habits you might have.

Bearing that in mind, here is a brief description of what a codependent relationship looks like:

- At least one person is suffering from some pathological condition
  - Most often that condition is narcissistic personality disorder or a drug addiction.

- One person (the codependent person) is being controlled or manipulated by the other one and the codependent person feels a strong need to be controlled by someone.

- Alternatively, one person (the codependent person) feels a strong need to have someone dependent upon him or her.

- Some of the more common symptoms of codependency include:
    - Denial
    - Low self esteem
    - Patterns of control
    - Excessively passive behavior or excessively complying with the wishes and demands of others (i.e.- a "push over")

The first understandings of codependency come out of what we know about alcoholism. It was in the treatment steps outlined by Alcoholics Anonymous that we first saw an attempt to address the fact that the problem of addiction goes far beyond the actual addict. A huge factor in absolutely any psychological condition includes the relationships in which the affected individual is involved.

Codependency is very similar to an earlier condition known as passive dependent personality disorder. However, the latter condition has fallen out of favor as the concept of codependency much more clearly emphasizes the role of relationships and social networks.

It is important to understand that some level of caretaking and self sacrifice are involved in the maintenance of any relationship. Every partnership involves a certain give and take. Defining the line between healthy and normal self sacrifice and codependency is difficult to do in a universalizing way. That is, it will be different for everybody and for each circumstance.

For example, a mother may need to sacrifice a lot in order to care for a child who suffers from a severe disability. The excess sacrifice does not necessarily mean the mother is codependent since her situation requires more caretaking than others.

In the most generalized terms, then, the problem of codependency is identified when the person consistently puts the needs of all (or many) others before his or her own. They have difficulty being alone and have an overwhelming desire to be constantly needed by someone. Thus, the difference between the mother with a disabled child and a codependent person is that the mother would be happy to see her child suddenly able to live and thrive on its own whereas the codependent person would attempt to keep the child in a state of needing constant care and assistance.

There is much more to be said on this topic in order to better understand how codependency is defined and diagnosed. We will discuss the definition in greater detail in later chapters. For now, this overview should be enough to give you a general idea of what this book is dealing with.

As a quick exercise, try to identify people you know who may be codependent. What habits or traits of this person led you to make that decision? Can you see connections between any problems that person tends to have with those codependent traits?

As another exercise, try to think about any codependent habits you might have. This does not necessarily mean you are fully codependent but there may be a few things that sound familiar to you or that you might have caught yourself doing or thinking.

Overview of the Book

In this book, you will read some important information about codependency. Topics that will be covered include:

- Recognizing codependency in yourself
- General signs of codependency
- General signs of an unhealthy relationship
- How codependency can be damaging to your relationship
- The problems which develop from codependency

- The consequences of ignoring the problem
- Step by step guide on overcoming codependency
- Tips for getting through the process of overcoming this problem
- Recognizing when you are finally no longer codependent
- Understanding and Achieving emotional intelligence
- General signs of a healthy relationship
- Common mistakes people make while working to overcome codependency
- Tips for avoiding those mistakes
- Tips for staying strong throughout this difficult journey

It is the goal of this book to provide everything you need to know in order to get started on your journey toward an improved, happier self: from recognizing the signs of codependency to taking those first steps to overcoming the problem. This book will guide you through the process and provide you with a great resource to rely on throughout.

With that in mind, however, it is beyond this book to provide a complete, comprehensive guide to overcoming codependency and you simply cannot overcome such a deep rooted problem simply by reading a book. You should seek out as many outside resources as possible.

So, while this book can't be your *only* guide through the process, it can give you a good idea of where to start and where to go next. If you are just getting started on the path of healing, you have come to the right place.

Chapter 1: How to Recognize Codependency

Recognizing codependency in yourself is one of the most difficult things to do. This has to do with a few different factors. First of all, it can be difficult to tell the difference from normal caretaking and healthy levels of self sacrifice and abnormal, unhealthy sacrifice and codependency. Second of all (and most importantly) it can be very hard to acknowledge a problem in yourself. But, recognizing the problem is the first step to happiness.

Before deciding one way or the other about whether or not you are codependent, continue reading through the rest of this book, doing the exercises and answering the questions as honestly as possible.

The Codependency Quiz

Since it can be very easy to dismiss a list of signs and symptoms; thinking that they do not necessarily apply to you; this chapter will begin with a quiz that will help you better assess where you are. After you have done the quiz, you can move on and read the signs of codependency with a more firm grasp or awareness of what sort of emotional state you are in. With that said, answer each question as honestly as possible. Right now, it is just you and this book so you won't have to share your answers with anyone else if you don't feel comfortable doing so.

1. On a scale of 1 to 5 (with 1 being not at all concerned and 5 being completely devastated), how upset are you when someone you care about has a negative opinion of you?

   a. 1 (0 points)
   b. 2 (1 point)
   c. 3 (2 points)
   d. 4 (3 points)
   e. 5 (4 points)

2. If you think you have done something very well but then someone else tells you that you have done a bad job or criticizes you, how do you feel?

    a. I know that I am still right and that their criticism is always completely unwarranted. (0 points)
    b. I doubt my own confidence in how well I've done and try to look at the situation from their perspective. (3 points)
    c. I try to understand their perspective to see if they might have a point, but overall, I trust in my own ability and know when I have done a good job. (2 points)

3. My family has a history of addiction (such as drugs or alcohol).

    a. True (4 points)

b. False (2 points)

c. Not Sure/ I don't know (0 points)

4. On a scale of 1 to 5 (with 1 being not at all concerned and 5 being completely devastated), how upset are you when you make a mistake?

   a. 1 (0 points)
   b. 2 (1 point)
   c. 3 (2 points)
   d. 4 (3 points)
   e. 5 (4 points)

5. I spend so much time dealing with other peoples' problems that I have little to no time left for myself.

   a. True (3 points)
   b. False (1 point)
   c. Not sure/ I don't know (0 points)

6. When I receive compliments from others, I feel:

    a. Grateful but I do not really believe them and take them to heart. (2 points)
    b. Grateful and I accept them when I know that they are based in truth. (1 point)
    c. Uncomfortable. I do not like getting compliments at all. (4 points)

7. For me, expressing myself and my true emotions is:

    a. Very easy. (2 points)
    b. Sometimes easy, sometimes more difficult. (1 point)
    c. Not something I like doing but I will if I have to. (3 points)

    d. Very difficult, sometimes almost impossible. (4 points)

8. In most cases, I prefer to just agree or stay quiet rather than deal with an argument.

    a. True (3 points)
    b. False (1 point)
    c. Not Sure/ I don't know (2 points)

9. I live to help and take care of others. If I did not have anyone to take care of, I would feel lost or aimless.

    a. True (4 points)
    b. False (1 point)
    c. Not Sure/ I don't know (2 points)

10. If I am not in control of a situation, I feel:

a. Helpless and sometimes even afraid. (3 points)
b. Anxious, but I try to adapt. (2 points)
c. Not really bothered. (1 point)

11. When my partner wants to spend time with friends rather than me, I feel:

a. Rejected or ignored. (4 points)
b. Disappointed but I accept that it has to happen sometimes. (3 points)
c. Understanding. I also like to have my time with friends, as well. (2 points)

12. I try very hard in everything I do to be pleasing to others so as not to cause pain or upset.

a. True (4 points)
b. False (2 points)
c. Not Sure/ I don't know (0 points)

13. I often doubt whether or not I am capable of achieving my goals or being truly happy.

   a. True (3 points)
   b. False (0 points)
   c. Not Sure/ I don't know (2 points)

14. I am always loyal to others, even if the other person has done something to hurt me.

   a. True (3 points)
   b. False (2 points)
   c. Not Sure/ I don't know (1 point)

15. I have difficulty refusing help to people if they ask for it.

    a. True (4 points)
    b. False (2 points)
    c. Not Sure/ I don't know (3 points)

16. I have difficulty trusting others or depending on them for my own needs.

    a. True (3 points)
    b. False (2 points)
    c. Not Sure/ I don't know (1 point)

17. I have a hard time dealing with change.

    a. True (3 points)
    b. False (2 points)
    c. Not Sure/ I don't know (1 point)

18. My partner or friends often tell me that I get jealous too easily.

    a. True (3 points)
    b. False (1 point)
    c. Not Sure/ I don't know (2 points)

19. I feel as if most people cannot take care of themselves and will always need help.

    a. True (4 points)
    b. False (1 point)
    c. Not Sure/ I don't know (2 points)

20. I find it difficult to accept help or advice from others.

    a. True (3 points)
    b. False (1 point)
    c. Not Sure/ I don't know (2 points)

The Codependency Quiz Results

Now that you have taken the quiz and, hopefully, answered each of the questions as honestly as you can, go back through and add all your points together. Then find which range you fall into and see if it sounds like you.

Between 57 and 70 points: Codependent Personality

If you fell within this range, there is a strong chance that you are codependent or, at the very least, are exhibiting many strong symptoms of codependency. These habits can interfere in your life in a number of ways so it is a good idea to try and work on them as soon as possible. Luckily, with this book in hand (or on your e-reader or if you are listening to it on audio), you are already have everything you need to get started.

Codependent personality is actually very common so you should not feel at all ashamed about this. And chances are, if you are exhibiting so many symptoms of codependency, you have a partner who is a dominant, manipulative personality. This is a dangerous line to walk as such people can be very abusive and the combination of a codependent person and a manipulative person quickly turns into a vicious cycle of emotional (and sometimes even physical) abuse. So it is important to stay aware and stay strong.

If you got this result, you may have to make some very tough decisions soon. But don't worry, change is possible and you are guaranteed to make a happier and more fulfilling future for yourself if you take the steps now to overcome your codependency. Becoming independent does not mean you have to become isolated and lonely. In fact, it means just the opposite. You will have the emotional strength to build real, meaningful relationships with people that will make you feel supported, loved, and secure. This is far better than any instant gratification you get from feeling constantly needed by others.

Between 43 and 56 points: Partially Codependent Personality

If you scored somewhere in this range, there is still more introspective work to be done. You may be at least partially codependent or you may simply be in a situation that brings out certain codependent traits. On the other hand, you may be completely fine and just suffering some temporary or mild insecurities which everyone experiences at one time or another.

No matter what the case may be for you, do not worry. There is a solution and there is a way to get yourself back to place of happiness and security. It would be a good idea to read through the rest of this chapter and then come back and take the quiz again when you are better informed about what each of the codependent traits mean.

In many cases, it is difficult to clearly see exactly what you are doing and what situation you are in while you are in the middle of it. So use this book as an excuse to take some meaningful time to reflect on your life and yourself. Find out if you might be a little more codependent than you were originally willing to admit or if you are just a little more insecure at the moment.

And whatever you decide, you may want to take a hard look at your relationship because chances are, if you are reading this right now, there are some problems that have popped up which have led you to have some doubts. Don't dismiss those doubts simply because you haven't found the answer yet. Dig deeper and try to really understand what is going on.

Between 29 and 42 points: No Codependent Traits

If your answers landed somewhere in this range, that is very good news. You probably are a very independent and healthy individual as far as your emotional life is concerned. However, if you have decided to take the time to read this book, there is a good chance something is amiss in your life at the moment. You shouldn't ignore this just because it can't be attributed to any tangible emotional disorder. Normal, well-functioning adults also have emotional distress and relationship problems. No one is immune.

So use this book as an opportunity to dig deeper into the nature of your relationship. Learn what the difference between healthy and unhealthy relationships are and learn the difference between healthy and unhealthy stress and disagreements that can occur in those relationships. Being in a committed relationship involves a lot of hard work so it is easy for it to fall off track once in a while. But remain hopeful. These problems have a solution and if you are willing to put in the time and energy to identify the exact problem and work toward a meaningful solution with your partner, you can once again find that happiness and joy that once made the relationship so wonderful. There is a lot of useful information in this book even for people who are not necessarily at the extreme of codependency.

Between 15 and 28 points: Some Narcissistic Tendencies

A score that landed in this range could be a warning sign for very different reasons. If you fell in this range, there is a chance that you are not the codependent one in the relationship but the dominant, manipulative person who is controlling the codependent partner. Of course, one quiz cannot tell you for sure that this is the case but if you got this result, it is worth taking the time to reflect and consider this option.

If you feel that you may have some of these narcissistic tendencies which usually attract codependent personalities, you should start working immediately toward healing yourself and becoming a more emotionally stable person. There are treatment options available and you and your partner can work together to overcome these problems.

For your part, it is still a good idea to read through the information in this book so that you can better understand the situation your partner might be in. Work on empathizing with his or her needs and avoiding using any of the manipulative tricks that seem to have worked so well in the past. You may not even be fully conscious of the fact that you have been manipulative or controlling but that's ok. As long as you make the effort to be aware now and change your behavior, there is still hope of building your relationship into something strong and healthy; something that can bring happiness and fulfillment to both of you.

Signs You Are Codependent

There are some key signs that can indicate whether or not a person is codependent. Knowing these signs can help you better assess your own situation. So read through them carefully and take note of the ones that stand out for you. Also, while reading through these signs, do not only think about yourself. Think about your partner as well.

It is impossible to think of codependency on individual terms as it can only appear in the context of a relationship. Furthermore, if there is any chance that it is your partner who is the codependent one (or that both of you have codependent tendencies), then it is absolutely essential that you recognize this fact as early as possible.

One more important thing to note before you get started: to be codependent does not mean that the person shows *all of these signs*. But if you or your partner show many of them and if those symptoms are fairly severe, there is a very strong chance you are (or your partner is) codependent. With that said, here are the most common signs of codependency:

- You have low self-esteem: you often feel that you are not quite good enough and you compare yourself to others. When you are alone with your thoughts, you tend to only think negative things about yourself. When you receive a compliment, you tend to dismiss it as simple flattery without any truth behind it. In order to compensate for your low self-esteem, you feel a constant need to help others or make yourself useful to them. When you do not feel needed, you lose most of your sense of self value.

- You have a habit of people pleasing: it's not a bad thing to want to make people happy. And no one will argue different. But people-pleasing becomes a problem when you find it difficult to say no to people even when you would otherwise want to. You end up sacrificing much more of yourself than you would really want to just to make sure that others are happy with you. You also have difficulty dealing with criticism (even constructive criticism) and if someone has a bad opinion of you, you tend to obsess or brood over this and can even become depressed or anxious.

- You have a fear of rejection: at the root of people-pleasing behavior is a fear of rejection. You are afraid that if you do stand up for yourself or say no to someone, they might be repelled by that and abandon you. You have extreme difficulty taking risks, no matter how substantial the reward could be because the fear of being rejected is far more overwhelming than the desire to make something more of yourself.

- You put the needs of your partner or the needs of the relationship above your own: you sacrifice yourself to a dangerous extreme just in order to make your partner happy or ensure that the relationship will hold together. You wear yourself out and neglect your own needs so that you can put as much as energy as possible into pleasing your partner. In fact, taking care of your own needs causes you to feel selfish. You would prefer to neglect yourself than be seen as selfish in any way.

- You have difficulty expressing your emotions: admitting how you truly feel to another person is a daunting task for you. And even when you really would want to express yourself, you find it difficult to do so because you are so out of practice and because you fear that the other person would misinterpret what you have said. You would rather bottle up your emotions than risk being misunderstood or made vulnerable.

- You have difficulty identifying your emotions: just as you can't really express your feelings to others, you also have difficulty understanding them yourself sometimes. Whether it's because you seem to have become angry or afraid out of nowhere or because you just aren't quite sure what it is your feeling. You sometimes feel confused and frustrated, unable to know what is really wrong even if without the pressure of saying it out loud.

- You let people take advantage of you: because you have difficulty saying no and you feel selfish taking care of your own needs; you often let others take advantage of you. As much as it distresses you, you would rather be taken advantage of than be seen as someone who takes advantage of others. Although you would like your partner to show the same consideration for you that you show for him or her, you would never dream of coming right out and asking for it.

- You often feel guilty or ashamed: you feel as if you can't remember the last time you *didn't* feel guilty or ashamed. Whether it is because you did something that made you feel that guilt or shame or because someone else did something that you think *they* should feel guilty or ashamed about. You often feel embarrassed for others when they are in embarrassing situations. And you tend to dwell on past moments of guilt, harboring the guilt you felt over things that happened years ago.

- You have difficulty trusting others: even when the person has given you no cause to distrust them, you still find it hard to really trust him or her. No matter how genuine they claim to be, you are afraid of letting yourself become completely vulnerable to anyone. You may not even be able to remember the last time you really trusted anyone. You feel much safer living a life of skepticism and keeping yourself at arm's length from everyone in order to protect yourself.

- You are a perfectionist: you hold yourself up to a very high standard—much higher than your standard for anyone else. You want to do everything you do perfectly and you want to be perfect at everything. Anything less than that and you feel like a complete failure. This high standard contributes to your low self-esteem. This is because if your standard is set at complete perfection in order to feel confident in yourself, then you are never going to have a chance to feel confident because no one is perfect. *No one.*

Signs of an Unhealthy Relationship

Beyond recognizing the key signs of codependency in yourself (or in your partner), it is also important to recognize the key signs of an unhealthy relationship in general. Sometimes it is easier to recognize the problems outside of yourself before you can recognize the ones inside. So after reading carefully through this list, go back through the previous section to see if some of the signs of codependency start hitting a little closer to home in your second read through.

- At least one person in the relationship is an addict (whether it's too drugs, alcohol, sex, gambling, work, or even food).

- You have experienced emotional, physical, or sexual abuse at the hands of your partner.

- You have done things that could be considered emotional, physical, or sexual abuse to your partner

- The communication line between you and your partner is almost or completely broken. You feel a widening gap between the two of you so that you feel unable to express your feelings or unable to know what your partner is truly feeling.

- Your partner always needs to be in control of the situation and if you try to make a suggestion or take even a little bit of control over something, he or she becomes enraged.

- You always feel the need to be in control of the situation and become extremely anxious or even angry when you feel that you have lost that control.

- Your partner has caused you serious pain (whether it is emotional, physical, or sexual) and you continue to remain loyal despite this.

- You feel as if you put all the effort into maintaining the relationship only to see that your partner puts absolutely no effort in and doesn't seem to care.

- Your partner often criticizes you or puts you down and you don't feel strong enough or worthy enough to defend yourself.

- Despite the frustration, anger, or pain that you feel as a result of your partner's behavior; you are afraid to leave for fear of being alone or unneeded.

Chapter 2: Problems and Consequences of Codependency

In reading through the last chapter, it might have already started to become clear to you what the problems and consequences of codependency could be. But not all of the consequences are so obvious or glaring. So this chapter is important because it will help to clarify some of the ones that might seem more obvious as well as point out some of the less obvious ones. Read through these carefully so that you are thoroughly informed and knowledgeable about the issues.

- Gateway to more serious problems: when codependency is left unresolved, it will often lead to serious problems that could be detrimental to your health and wellbeing. Codependent people are at an extremely high risk for becoming alcoholics and drug addicts later in life. They are also at a higher risk for developing eating disorders and other self-destructive behaviors. And you are at an even higher risk or developing these problems if you are with someone who currently has one of these problems (such as an alcoholic or drug addict).

- Continued abuse or stress: those who suffer from codependency are significantly more likely to remain in abusive or stressful situations regardless of the emotional, physical, or other damage it is causing to them. They may · remain in an abusive relationship or, if they have gotten out of an abusive relationship but failed to resolve the deep rooted codependency issues, they may attract another abusive partner. Codependent people are also more likely to keep working at a stressful and unfulfilling job without bothering to try and find something better. They are also significantly less likely to seek medical attention even when they really need it.

- Less successful in their careers: this may not seem like an obvious consequence at first but the fact of the matter is that codependent people are much less likely to be successful in their chosen career path. They typically earn less money than others in their same position and they are much less likely to get promoted. This has to do with a number of factors including low self-esteem; guilt and shame associated with making any sort of demand (even reasonable demands); a crippling fear of being rejected; and a general unwillingness to take any sort of risks.

- Development of full mental or personality disorders: when not dealt with and left not resolved, codependency will often progress into other, even more serious problems. The low self-esteem and fear of being rejected when left unchecked can lead to problems such as severe social anxiety, certain social phobias, or even avoidant personality disorder. Stress related disorders such as panic disorder, posttraumatic stress disorder or even depression are also very common.

- Serious damage to physical health: like some of the other problems mentioned so far, this one might not seem obvious at first. However, there is a wide variety of health problems that can result from codependency and codependent behavior. This problem is made worse by the fact that codependent people are less likely to get the medical care they require. Common health problems found in codependent people include high blood pressure, respiratory problems, heart problems, ulcers and headaches among many others. Indirectly, codependent people can suffer from poor health due to physical abuse perpetrated by the partner or the onset of an addiction or other self-destructive habit.

- Enabling negative behaviors or habits: codependency leads to caring for other people to an unhealthy degree. You will let emotional, physical, or even sexual abuse go unchecked in order to avoid being abandoned by your partner. If he or she has an addiction, you will—through your caretaking—encourage this addiction. That is not to say that you do so constantly but by refusing to express your concern or show tough love, you allow the addiction to continue. In not caring about your own needs, you allow your partner's aggressive or otherwise inappropriate behavior to continue no matter how much it harms you.

- Teaching codependency by example: if you and your partner have children, the consequences of codependency go far beyond you. If either you or your partner are codependent, your children will learn those same unhealthy behaviors by watching you and your partner interact. As they grow up, they will internalize these things and likely become codependent themselves. Therefore, leaving your own issues unresolved does not just damage your own health and that of your partner's, it will also hurt your children in the long run. So if you don't feel as if you have the strength to overcome your codependency for your own self-fulfillment and happiness; do it for your children.

These are only a few of the more common problems and consequences of codependency. The list could be much longer and much more in depth. But the focus of this book is not to scrutinize every possible consequence. Rather, this book will focus on healing and overcoming your codependency. Therefore, the rest of the chapters are dedicated to information about how to overcome your problems and how to recognize and acknowledge the progress you are making.

Chapter 3: Steps to Overcoming Codependency

One of the most important things to do in order to overcome codependency is to get informed. You need to know what sort of beast you are dealing with and what the best way to tackle it is. In reading this book, you have already begun that process of getting informed. As you have probably already noticed from reading the earlier chapters of this book, there is a lot to learn and a lot you need to stay aware of.

No one is going to tell you that this will be an easy process. It is going to be difficult. Especially at the beginning when you are just starting out. What you can be confident in, however, is that it will get easier and easier with time. Each step you successfully complete will make you that much stronger and that much more capable of moving on to the next step.

It is important to assess your limits and understand what your strengths and weaknesses in this current moment are. The steps to overcoming codependency which you will read below are not necessarily in the correct order for you. Rearrange them in any way you see fit. Start with whatever seems most manageable for you and work from there.

The important thing is not doing it in the exact order listed here but *doing* it all. As you accomplish each of the things on this list (in whichever order you choose to accomplish them), you will soon begin to notice a positive change in yourself. Stay aware of that and be willing to acknowledge it. The more you notice this change, the more confident you will become in your ability to successfully change.

Above all, it is important to remember that while it would be great if your partner made changes as well (as he or she is definitely contributing to the problem), the most important thing here is to focus on yourself. That may seem difficult now when you are so used to neglecting yourself for the sake of others. But at this stage, think of it in terms you can understand: you are focusing on improving yourself so that you can be a healthier, more positive person for others. Be a positive role model for children or peers. Be a happier person so that those around you are made happier just by your presence.

How to Overcome Your Codependency

- Assess your present situation: this step is important because it will let you know where your starting off point is. Use the quiz in chapter 1 and the information in all the previous chapters to help you think as objectively as possible about where you currently are in life. Ask yourself the following questions and allow yourself to answer honestly. Write them down if it will help you better see and organize your thoughts and emotions:

- How often do I feel *truly* and *deeply* happy?
- How much of my day do I spend filled with anxiety, fear, or anger?
- Is my current life situation where I imagined myself to be?
- Is this where I really want to be in life?
- What does my *ideal* life look like?
- What characteristics and traits does my *ideal* partner have?
- And how many of those traits does my current partner actually have?
- When are the times that I feel or felt the most happy?
- What would I be doing right now if I were not in a relationship?
- If I could go back in time and give my childhood self some advice, what would it be?

- Understand what led to this situation: you cannot ever truly understand the present without understanding the past events that led up to it. Take the time to reflect on your past: your childhood, your teenage years, and your young adult life. Understanding the past events that led up to the present will help you to better understand both when and how the problems began to occur which will put you in a much better position to resolve the problems. Ask yourself the following questions to help you think about your past:

  - What memory or memories stick out the most to me? (memories of happiness, sadness, tragedy, mistakes, lessons learned, etc)
  - What is it about this memory or memories that are so striking?
  - How did I act when I was younger?

- How does that differ from the way I am now?
- How did my partner act when we first met?
- How does that differ from the way he or she acts now?
- What memories do I have of my parents (or the people who raised you and played that role)?
- Reflecting back, did either of them show signs of codependency?

- Visualize a better future: up until now, you have looked at the present and past. Now it is time to turn your gaze toward the future. Visualize a future in which you are happy (not your partner, not your friends, not your boss, you). Let your imagination go a little with this one. You don't have to worry about what is and is not possible at this current moment. The important thing is visualizing and

knowing what you would want for your
future.

- What does that future look like?
- What are you doing?
- Where do you live?
- How do you act?
- What sort of hobbies or interests
  do you have?
- What kind of people are you
  surrounded with?

- Make a bucket list: make a list of
  everything you would want to do before
  you die. Have you ever wanted to travel?
  Learn a foreign language? Write a book of
  poems? Climb Mount Everest? Write
  everything you have ever wanted to do
  down and read over the list a couple
  times.
  If you can, keep this list somewhere safe
  at all times. You can come back to it and

add more things as you think of them. Making a bucket list is a healthy activity because, regardless of whether or not you manage to accomplish every single thing on the list, it is good to have a concrete reference of your own personal dreams and aspirations that are all your own and independent of anyone else.

Your bucket list is a list of the things you want to do for your own pleasure. Just knowing that you have such a list will help remind you that you are an independent person outside of any relationship you are currently in.

• Admit you are codependent: this step is not listed first on purpose. In most cases, it is very difficult to admit your problem until you take the time reflect on yourself and your situation or try to do something that a person without the problem would easily be able to do. It is not easy to admit to being codependent. And, in reality, this is not one step. Admitting this is a multi-step process in itself.

First, you need to admit to yourself that you are codependent. Accept this fact fully and thoroughly on your own without telling anyone else. Once you have accepted this yourself, admit you are codependent to someone else. Do not admit it to your partner yet (since he or she is part of your problem) but choose a close friend or relative that you can confide in. Admit it to them one on one, in a calm setting.

If you can't think of any person in your life you would feel safe confiding in, get a therapist and admit it to him or her. After these first two steps are complete, you can slowly work on admitting your codependency to other important people in your life.

- Seek out therapy: getting a therapist can help make this entire process a million times easier. So don't be afraid to look for a nearby therapist. And don't just stick with the first one you find (unless you feel an immediate connection with the person). Try out a few different therapists and stay with the one you feel the most comfortable with. Therapists are trained and experienced professionals in emotional problems and will be able to give you the best and most personalized advice about how to overcome your own issues.

- Find a support group: there are lots of support groups out there designed to help specific kinds of people. From Alcoholics

Anonymous to cancer survivors, there is a support group for everything. Look for a support group focused on codependency.

Even if you just go and don't say a word at first, just being there and listening to others talk about their own experiences will help you to feel less isolated and alone in your own problems. And you may also be able to learn from their experiences and mistakes. The more you attend, the easier it will become to start opening up and sharing yourself. And when this happens, you will be a huge step closer to overcoming your codependency.

- Fight negativity with positivity: in order to help battle the low self-esteem that often comes with codependency, you need to fight the negativity with positivity. That is, for each negative thought that you have, counter it with a positive thought. Even if the positive thought is something much smaller than the negative one, getting in this habit will help you slowly build a much more balanced and realistic picture of yourself.

For example, if you make a mistake and criticize yourself for having done something wrong; counter that thought by finding something which you have done right. As you get more and more practiced at this and it becomes a regular habit, you will find yourself having more and more positive thoughts without even having to try. You will become better and better at noticing the things you (and others) are good at or do well.

This will help encourage and motivate you to continue on your healing journey. Not to mention, it is a small and simple enough step that you can start this without having to make any major or noticeable changes in your life. The changes will come on their own as you get better and better at thinking positively.

- Express yourself somehow: in order to improve your ability to communicate your thoughts and feelings, you have to practice. Unfortunately, there's no easy trick to doing this. You simply have to start small. Express thoughts or feelings that you still feel relatively safe expressing.

Express your distaste for a certain food, for example. Slowly build up to bigger and more important emotions. This is not a single step but a long, drawn out process. It is going to take time. Most likely, this will take more time than any of the others. But you have to start sometime and sooner is better than later.

Make an effort every single day to express at least one thought or emotion that you might not have otherwise said anything about. Note people's reactions to what you have said. In particular, note how much less dramatic and terrifying it turned out to be. You expressed something and everyone around you still likes you and talks to you. It's going to be ok.

- Cut off toxic ties: this is another one of the more difficult steps and it sort of presents you with a catch 22. On the one hand, the recovery process will be much easier if you cut all the toxic people from your life right from the get go. But, on the other hand, when you are in the depths of your codependency issues, it can seem nearly impossible to find the strength to completely cut those people off who are feeding your codependency.

So, while the solution to this paradox will be different for every individual, a general rule of thumb might be: if the toxic person hasn't yet gotten to the point of physical or sexual abuse, you can delay this step until you are a little stronger.

However, if you are being physically or sexually abused, you need to get out of the relationship now, no matter how impossible it may seem. Make sure to consult your therapist about this issue as he or she will be able to provide the best advice for how to deal with your unique circumstances.

- Take up hobbies and interests: this one is an easier step. You can either take up an old hobby that you somehow lost touch with or find new interests and passions to pursue. The most important thing, however, is that this hobby or interest be something you do on your own—not with your partner or any other toxic people in your life.

Go out and sign up for a woodshop class at the local community center or buy a book full of recipes you have never cooked before. Whatever interests you most, go out and do it. Having hobbies and interests that you can do independently of any one in your life will keep you grounded and remind you that you are an independent person, capable of living and thriving even outside of any relationship.

- Start saying no: this one, like the step about expressing yourself, has no special trick. It simply takes practice. Start by saying no to very small things. If your partner asks if you want to watch a TV show you don't really want to watch, say no.

Make an effort to say no to at least one request asked of you per day—even if it is something you otherwise would not mind doing. By starting small, you can reassure yourself that denying your help will cause no great burden to the other person. Someone can just easily get their own cup of coffee from the kitchen as you can. The more you say no and realize that the world does not, in fact, end as a result, the easier it will become to say no to the things that actually matter.

- Know the difference between selfishness and emotional maturity: this step is not so easy to describe. But you need to work on understanding that the steps you are taking are not intended to make you a selfish person, in fact, in following them correctly, you will become a less selfish person since you will not falsely believe that everyone depends solely on you or that everyone concerns themselves 100% of the time with what you are doing wrong. Realizing that you need to take care of your own needs before you are even truly capable of taking care of anyone else's needs is one of the most important truths you can learn.

Chapter 4: More Tips and Advice for Overcoming Codependency

Aside from the main steps listed in the previous chapter, there are few smaller things you can start doing to help make the process a little easier. As you do these small things more and more, they will eventually grow into habits and once they are habits, they can help construct your emotional foundations. You do not need to do every single one of these things. In fact, some of them may not even work very well for you. These tips are more intended as suggestions and guidance. Let them inspire you to develop your own positive habits.

- Keep a journal: writing a journal is an excellent way to make the whole process of self-reflection a lot easier. You can use it as a reference and memory aid. And reading what you wrote a few days after the fact will help you to better reflect on what happened and how you actually felt in that moment. This will prevent you from minimizing pain you have felt in the past and from over dramatizing smaller events. So as you write, remember to write down both what happened and what you feel. Getting in this habit will also help you to get better at identifying your feelings (something that many codependent personalities struggle with).

• Do something creative: creative activities can be immensely therapeutic and relaxing. It can also help give your subconscious emotions a means of expression. When you don't know how to say what you are feeling in words (or aren't even sure yourself what you are feeling), doing something creative can help you process those emotions in alternate ways. Plus, you will end up with something cool in the end. So whether it's arts, crafts, or some sort of DIY project, take the time every week to do something creative. Who knows? You may discover some hidden talents in yourself. At the very least, you will discover some hidden emotions.

- Make To Do Lists: this might seem like it is coming out of left field but To Do lists can help more than you think. Each morning (or each evening before you go to bed), make a To Do list for the day. Include big important tasks as well as the little things. As you complete each task throughout the day, mark it off your list. This is a positive habit that will help you better realize just how much you really do get done in a day. It is a wonderful feeling to sit down after a long day and look at a long list full of completed tasks.

- Set one small goal for each day: working from the list of steps to recovery in the previous section, set a recovery goal for yourself each day. Whether it is expressing a thought, saying no, finding a new hobby, or working on any of the other steps. Starting the day with the clear intention of how you plan to work on your recovery will not only help keep you on track but also help you notice the progress you are making. Think about it, after one week of doing this, you will have accomplished 7 goals that are helping your recovery. Add those 7 goals together and you are that much closer to recovery.

- Notice something beautiful: take the time every single day to stop and notice something beautiful or pleasant. It could be the sunset, a cute dog, a particularly artistic piece of graffiti, or even just an extra well-made sandwich eaten for lunch. Just remember to stop and take a moment to acknowledge how wonderful it is and let yourself just enjoy it without any outside pressure from anyone else. This is your own small moment of enjoyment and peacefulness that you can have all on your own without anybody else.

- Acknowledge an accomplishment: every single night, as you are going to sleep, think of at least one thing you accomplished that day. It could simply be accomplishing the small recovery goal you had set or it could be marking off everything on your To Do list. No matter how big or small, every accomplishment counts. As you are going to sleep, you can use that time to appreciate what you have accomplished. If you can think of more than one thing, go for it. But always come up with at least one accomplishment from your day.

- Keep a dream journal: each morning, as soon as you wake up, write down everything you can remember from your dreams. This can be fun and enlightening.

A dream journal will help you get more in touch with your subconscious and all those unexpressed emotions you are struggling with.

Plus, it can be an interesting way to pass the time to read through all the dreams you have been having the past few nights. As you reread them, look for any common symbols or themes. Alternatively, you can compare your dream journal with your regular day to day journal to see what in your life might be influencing your dreams. If you don't feel like an expert dream interpreter, you can take your dream journal (and your regular daily journal while you are at it) to your therapist to get his or her thoughts and opinions.

- Start up a savings for something you want: even if you do not have very much money to put away, this can be a very good exercise. Working toward a tangible long term goal like a vacation or a new dress can help you build emotional strength and endurance. So even if you are just putting leftover change from the day into a jar, start saving money. And start saving it for a specific goal.

Even if you do not feel comfortable telling anyone what exactly you are saving for, you can still build up a savings and know for yourself what your goal is. Let it be a somewhat long term goal, though such as a dream vacation or even just a fairly expensive piece of jewelry or other item that you want. Part of building up emotional strength is learning to appreciate delayed gratification and long term rewards. Saving up for things you want to get in the future can help you develop that skill.

With these steps and tips in mind, you are ready to begin your own journey to self-recovery. This is one of the most courageous and inspirational decisions you could have made so congratulate yourself for coming this far and for deciding that it is time to change. In the next chapter, you will learn how to recognize healthy behaviors and healthy relationships so that you will be better equipped to notice your own progress and improvements. This will keep you motivated and strong as you work through the process.

Chapter 5: How to Recognize When You Are No Longer Codependent

In the early chapters, you learned how to recognize negative behaviors and warning signs related to codependency and unhealthy relationships in general. Then, in chapter 3 and 4, you learned some strategies for how to recover from any codependent habits you may have. Now, the book will turn to focus on recognizing the good signs that show you are making progress and your relationships are getting healthier.

What is Emotional Intelligence?

Emotional Intelligence is the ability to clearly understand your own emotional state as well as the emotional state of others. This means you can accurately identify different emotions and understand what caused them or where they are coming from. If this sounds difficult, it is even harder.

Most people, whether they are considered normal and healthy or not, do not have perfect emotional intelligence. There is always a blind spot. There are certain emotions or triggers for emotions that a person is unable to recognize or fully understand. It takes a lot of practice and training in order to fully develop your emotional intelligence.

In order to better assess your own emotional intelligence, answer the questions in this short quiz as honestly as you can:

1. For the most part, I am always aware of how each of my friends feels toward other friends that are in our social circle.

    a. Strongly agree (4 points)
    b. Agree (3 points)
    c. Disagree (2 points)
    d. Strongly disagree (1 point)

2. When I feel anxious or upset, I usually know exactly what caused the feeling and when.

   a. Strongly agree (4 points)
   b. Agree (3 points)
   c. Disagree (2 points)
   d. Strongly disagree (1 point)

3. For the most part, I am happy with who I am right now. There might be one or two things I would like to change but overall, I am content with myself.

   a. Strongly agree (4 points)
   b. Agree (3 points)
   c. Disagree (2 points)
   d. Strongly disagree (1 point)

4. I become really frustrated and angry with myself whenever I make a mistake.

   a. Strongly agree (1 point)
   b. Agree (2 points)
   c. Disagree (3 points)
   d. Strongly disagree (4 points)

5. I try my best to avoid confrontation or intensely emotional situations.

   a. Strongly agree (1 point)
   b. Agree (2 points)
   c. Disagree (3 points)
   d. Strongly disagree (4 points)

6. Around new people, I am very closed off or present a different version of myself. I don't start opening up until I really know the person well.

a. Strongly agree (1 point)

b. Agree (2 points)

c. Disagree (3 points)

d. Strongly disagree (4 points)

7. If even the smallest thing goes wrong, I have a tendency to get really frustrated and upset. I need everything to go exactly right.

a. Strongly agree (1 point)

b. Agree (2 points)

c. Disagree (3 points)

d. Strongly disagree (4 points)

8. In general, I know what I can and cannot do and I am confident in my own talents and skills.

a. Strongly agree (4 points)

b. Agree (3 points)

c. Disagree (2 points)

d. Strongly disagree (1 point)

9. I feel that I am a good judge of a person's character. I have a natural instinct for these things.

   a. Strongly agree (4 points)
   b. Agree (3 points)
   c. Disagree (2 points)
   d. Strongly disagree (1 point)

10. When faced with a task I am really dreading, I usually:

    a. Just don't do anything at all. (1 point)
    b. Procrastinate and wait until the last minute. (2 points)
    c. Try to get it over with as quickly as possible. (3 points)

d. Create a manageable plan and work on the task little by little each day until it is done. (4 points)

11. When an argument gets really heated and intense, I usually:

    a. Call for a time out so that we can both take some time to think things over. (4 points)
    b. Give up and apologize even if I'm not at fault just so that the argument will end. (3 points)
    c. Resort to insulting the person (2 points)
    d. Shut down completely and stop responding. (1 point)

12. When I need to make a very important decision, I usually:

a. Go with my gut (4 points)
b. Get advice from others and follow it. (3 points)
c. Choose the easiest possible option. (2 points)
d. Choose randomly. (1 point)

13. In regard to your social life, which of the following statements most closely fits you:

a. Making friends is easy and I enjoy meeting all kinds of new people. (3 points)
b. I don't have trouble getting along with other people but I don't consider someone a true friend until I really get to know them. (4 points)
c. Meeting people and making friends is difficult for me. (2 points)

d. I have a lot of difficulty making friends. It is basically impossible for me. (1 point)

14. I am very open to change.

    a. Strongly agree (4 points)
    b. Agree (3 points)
    c. Disagree (2 points)
    d. Strongly disagree (1 point)

15. Whenever I receive criticism of any kind, I immediately become upset and defensive.

    a. Strongly agree (1 point)
    b. Agree (2 points)
    c. Disagree (3 points)
    d. Strongly disagree (4 points)

16. If I notice that an annoying habit of my partner seems to be getting worse, I will:

   a. Tell him or her exactly what is bothering me. (4 points)
   b. Complain about the annoying habit to other people. (2 points)
   c. Say nothing and just deal with it. (1 point)

17. When I am under a lot of pressure or very stressed out, I usually:

a. Become extremely anxious and obsess over all my problems. (3 points)
b. Feel overwhelmed and hopeless. (2 points)
c. Feel angry that no one is noticing how much pressure I am under. (3 points)
d. Become depressed and ready to give up. (1 point)

18. In general, I would say I am stressed or under a lot of pressure most of the time.

    a. Strongly agree (1 point)
    b. Agree (2 points)
    c. Disagree (3 points)
    d. Strongly disagree (4 points)

19. In most situations, expressing my honest opinions or feelings is easy for me.

    a. Strongly agree (4 points)
    b. Agree (3 points)
    c. Disagree (2 points)
    d. Strongly disagree (1 point)

20. I always make an effort to be aware of the moods of others and feel that I am usually good at knowing what other people are really feeling.

a. Strongly agree (4 points)
b. Agree (3 points)
c. Disagree (2 points)
d. Strongly disagree (1 point)

Quiz Results

- (60-79)Above Average Emotional Intelligence

If you scored with in this range, congratulations! You are a very emotionally intelligent and stable person. It takes a lot of work and high level of reasoning to achieve this so you should feel very proud of yourself. But emotional intelligence is not just something you have. You will always need to work to maintain it. Just like a body builder will eventually lose his strength when he stops working out, you will start to lose your emotional intelligence when you stop actively exercising it.

- (35-59)Average Emotional Intelligence

If you fell within this range, you, like most people have some emotional intelligence but struggle with a few difficult parts. Perhaps you handle stress and pressure poorly or perhaps you have difficulty acknowledging your negative emotions. Try to identify your weak points and what you have difficulties with and use the strategies described in chapter 3 in order to start working on those weak points and building up your emotional intelligence.

- (20-34)Below Average Emotional Intelligence

If your score fell within this range, you probably have a lot of difficulty dealing with emotional situations and even just dealing with your own emotions. If you are reading this book, you have come to the right place. With this book, you have all the tools necessary to get started on your journey to self-recovery. Even if you scored in this range, it does not mean you are a lost cause and will never be able to build up your emotional intelligence. It takes work and persistence no matter who you are. In fact, many people with high emotional intelligence once suffered from dangerously low levels of emotional intelligence. It was through the process of healing and strengthening themselves that they learned the skills and abilities that make them the strong, emotionally intelligent people they are today. That can be you, too, in the future!

Signs of a Healthy You

If your points fell within the upper end of the spectrum on the quiz above, that is one of the strongest indicators you are a healthy person emotionally. Make sure to save this book so that you can take the quiz again later on down the road after you have made more progress on your path of healing to see how much your score has improved. There are also many emotional intelligence quizzes to be found online so if you would like to get a more complete picture of your emotional intelligence, take a few different tests and see how well you do on average.

Beyond your emotional intelligence, there are some other more tangible signs that you are becoming emotionally healthier. Those signs include:

- You have hobbies and interests of your own: whether it's working out, reading, or doing arts and crafts, if you are able to enjoy spending quality time with yourself, doing things you like doing just for the sake of your enjoyment, this is a great sign you are a strong, happy person.

- You handle criticism with grace: whether its constructive criticism or just blatant insults, you can take any criticism with a grain of salt and handle it calmly and objectively. You realize that while other people may have some valid points; their opinions cannot really affect what you know to be true about yourself.

- You know your limits: you know how much stress you can handle and how much work you can take on at any one time. Of course, you cannot always control what life throws your way but you do your best not to let yourself go beyond your own limits. When it does happen, you do feel more stressed than usual but you bear through it and do your best to get everything done; knowing all the while that this is a temporary burden and things will soon return to their equilibrium.

- You express yourself well: you may not open up to everyone all the time and bluntly state your opinion in every single circumstance. But you do not hesitate to express your emotions articulately when the situation needs it. That is, you will not bottle up your emotions just to avoid confrontation or negative reactions. You know it is better to make your feelings known to the other person so that he or she understands where you are coming from.

Signs of a Healthy Relationship

Recognizing when you are in a healthy relationship is just as important as recognizing when you yourself are healthy. This is because you may be making dramatic improvements on your own emotional well being while your partner continues to brood and stagnate in a state of narcissism, addiction, codependency, or any other emotionally unhealthy state. If you can see some of the following signs in your relationship (or you can see noticeable progress toward them), you can be confident that you and your partner are on the right track.

- You make time for your friends and enjoy it: every once in awhile, you like to go out with your friends without your partner there. This is not because you don't love him or her. Rather, it is just nice sometimes to get out with your friends and have some quality time with people you aren't romantically involved with. And you also have no problem at all when your partner wants to do the same thing with his or her friends.

- You argue well: every relationship has its points of disagreement and less than perfect moments. But when these disagreements do come, you always treat each other with love and respect. You talk calmly and openly about your problems and listen intently to the concerns of your partner (and your partner does the same for you). When those inevitable moments come that you find it difficult to stay calm and monitor your emotions, you call for a time out and take some time to gather your thoughts and consider the situation more thoroughly before resuming the argument with your new perspective.

- You don't play games: between you and your partner, there is no need for manipulation, tricks, or threats in order to get what you want. You are open and honest with each other. If you want something, you will come right out and say it. And you trust that your partner will do the same. Your wants may come in conflict with each other at some points but that is alright. You are adept at discussing these conflicts in a constructive way so that you both can live happily and comfortably inside the relationship.

- The communication lines are always open: you never feel afraid to express yourself to your partner. You feel as if you can say anything and be as honest as you know how. You work to make sure that your partner feels the same way toward you. With the communication lines open, you know that problems will come up as soon as they arise so that the two of you can deal with them immediately rather than letting them fester and grow beneath the surface until they explode and become something completely unmanageable.

- You show each other that you love each other: this doesn't mean you bring each other gifts and chocolate every single day but you do make it known that you love and care for each other. You listen to what the other person says with genuine interest and you do everything you can to make your partner feel comfortable, safe, and loved (and your partner does the same for you).

- You do not expect perfection: both of you are very aware that nobody is perfect and you wouldn't want it any other way. You love your partner precisely because of the person he or she is, not the impossibly perfect person he or she could be. And your partner loves you for the same reasons. When arguments or disagreements do occur, it is never for frustration over failed perfection or lack of love. It is just a natural human occurrence that happens between two people and the two of you are able to handle it maturely and lovingly, knowing that after it is resolved you can go back to the happiness you regularly enjoy with each other.

Conclusion

With this book, you hopefully have learned all the information you need to know to get started on a healing path of recovery. Just reading the book alone is not enough to overcome your codependency. But, with the information contained in these pages, you have the tools necessary to get started.

Overcoming a problem like codependency is not easy but it also is not impossible. You have the strength within you; you just need to work on it. Achieving emotional intelligence and becoming a happy, healthy individual takes effort just as anything worth doing does.

Do not be overwhelmed by the road that lies ahead of you. Instead, focus on each individual step you are taking. As long as you are walking forward, no matter how small each step is, you are going in the right direction. And the more you progress, the easier it will get.

Be persistent and build up your strength. Keep this book with you so that you can refer to it when you need to. And above all else, remember that you can do it!

Other books available by author on Kindle, paperback and audio

Emotionally Abusive Relationships:

Identifying and Effectively Dealing with Narcissists, Sociopaths, Psychopaths and Toxic People

CPSIA information can be obtained at www.ICGtesting.com
Printed in the USA
BVOW08s1736271215

431105BV00001B/5/P